The incidence of loneliness among divorced adults.

Elsie S. Pearson

ABSTRACT

The purpose of this quantitative study is to explore factors contributing to loneliness among divorced adults. The current study examined demographic characteristics, smoking habits, mental health factors, disabilities, and their impact on loneliness among divorced adults. The 2020 California Health Interview Survey (CHIS) data was used for this study. The study found that the following demographic characteristics, race, education level, employment, and age are associated with loneliness. This study also found that smoking habits, caregiving, and disabilities are associated with loneliness. No statistically significant relationships were found regarding mental health factors such as hopelessness, depression, and worthlessness with loneliness. Being nervous and restless had a weak, negative association with loneliness.

ACKNOWLEDGEMENTS

As my graduate career ends, the individuals who have encouraged me and kept me grounded throughout this rigorous process need to be recognized. My fellow social work and mental health community members have fostered a confidence and love for the helping profession in me that I will hold onto for the rest of my career in serving our communities. In this program, I have made life-long connections that allowed me to endure the thesis process. I thank my cohort for their loving support that has pushed me to continue reflecting on my identities and to pursue my passion for serving vulnerable populations.

Dr. Janaki Santhiveeran, my thesis advisor, gave me and all her students more hours, compassion, and guidance than I can ever repay her. Because of her, I found the confidence to commit to completing such intensive research. Her ability to provide thorough guidance on quantitative analysis while seamlessly serving as a life mentor has inspired me. It will continue to be an experience of genuine gratitude for the rest of my life. I am also immensely grateful for the time and efforts given by the committee members. A special thank you goes out to all the wonderful, insightful, and resilient clients I have worked with during my graduate career. Each one of the individuals I had the honor to serve has left a unique and meaningful mark on my heart. Lastly, I would like to thank my partner for supporting me in all ways imaginable as I pursued my dreams. I hope to one day show up for all the individuals who helped me get here in the same ways they all did for me.

TABLE OF CONTENTS

LIST OF TABLES

CHAPTER 1

INTRODUCTION

Divorce can create significant stress levels among families and typically constitutes many challenges such as financial adjustments, parenting conflicts, and emotional disturbances (Sbarra et al., 2015). Issues in the areas of communication, trust, commitment, and sexual satisfaction are common predictors of divorce (Zineldin, 2019). Overall, divorce rates are slightly declining but continue to increase among individuals 50 years and older (Raley & Sweeney, 2020). A reduction in overall child well-being continues to be associated with parental divorce. Divorce can also contribute to the growing financial inequality between men and women because marriage dissolution has been shown to impact the financial aspect of women's lives more severely (Raley & Sweeney, 2020). A long-term problem for women after a divorce is the burden of single parenting (Leopold, 2018). For men, a long-term consequence of divorce is adverse health outcomes (Couch et al., 2015). Parental divorce also negatively impacts children into adulthood, including chronic emotional and behavioral issues (Tullius et al., 2021). Divorce also impacts individuals' social lives, drastically increasing the likelihood of loneliness (Van Tilburg et al., 2015).

Loneliness, the negative feeling associated with lacking social connectedness with others, can impact individuals at any age (Cacioppo et al., 2015). As the rates of loneliness rise, individuals experiencing loneliness are a concern (Chatterjee, 2018). Consequently, the National Academy of Medicine encourages clinicians to gather and monitor details regarding factors associated with loneliness (Mullen et al., 2019). Studies showed that various risk factors contribute to loneliness among individuals including education, finances, social networks, disabilities, physical well-being, and living situations (Clark et al., 2021; Hutten et al., 2021).

Those experiencing loneliness typically do not have close friends or family (Cacioppo et al., 2015). A Cigna study reveals that rates of loneliness increased from 54% of individuals reporting feeling lonely in 2018 to 61% in 2019 (The Cigna Group, 2022). Roughly one third of those 45 years old and above reported being lonely (Anderson, 2010). Loneliness is complex and individuals with similar social relationships may experience different levels of loneliness (Barreto et al., 2021). Considering that the United States has the highest divorce rate, which is about half of the marriages resulting in divorce, it is imperative that the factors contributing to the level of loneliness of this population be explored to consider effective interventions (Barreto et al., 2021; Mullen et al., 2019).

Divorce trends vary by age. Although the younger population remains more likely to divorce, recent trends show that the rates of more youthful individuals are decreasing while the rates of divorce in the older population rise (Cohen, 2019; Raley & Sweeney, 2020). Women of Asian ethnicities and immigrant Hispanic women are less likely to divorce than Hispanic women born in the United States and Native American women (Raley & Sweeney, 2020). Men have more drastic decreases in life satisfaction in the first year after a divorce than women, but over the years, there is little difference in life satisfaction among divorced men and women (Leopold, 2018). Divorce is emotionally taxing and administratively daunting with overcrowded dockets, lengthy waiting periods, legal costs, and custody battles (Munro et al., 2016).

Along with immense impacts on the adults experiencing divorce, children of divorced parents are also at risk for mental health problems (Boring et al., 2015) because divorced parents assign self-blame for the parental conflict which negatively impacts a child's quality of life (Sorek, 2019). The Institute for Family Studies (n.d.) recognizes the wide range of effects caused by divorce. It describes how to prevent divorce, cope with blended families, impacts on children, and the family law system (Institute for Family Studies, n.d). According to the Centers for Disease Control and Prevention (CDC; 2021c), loneliness can make older adults 50% more likely to experience dementia. The National Academies of Sciences, Engineering, and Medicine (2020) also report that loneliness is associated with higher hospitalizations and premature death.

Purpose of the Study

This study examines factors contributing to the level of loneliness among divorced adults. The study explored demographic characteristics, smoking habits, mental health factors, disabilities, and their impact on loneliness.

Research Questions

The study explored the following questions:

1. Is there a relationship between demographic characteristics (race, age, gender, work status, and education) and loneliness among divorced adults?

2. Is there a relationship between smoking habits (current and frequency) and the level of loneliness among divorced adults?

3. Is there a relationship between caregiving (whether or not provided care, financial stress due to caregiving, suffered physical or mental health due to caregiving, relationship to care recipient, whether or not living with the care recipient, and providing care for dementia) and the level of loneliness among divorced adults?

4. Is there a relationship between mental health (hopelessness, nervousness, restlessness, depression, and worthlessness) and loneliness among divorced adults?

5. Is there a relationship between disabilities (blind/deaf/severe loss of sight/hearing and diabetes) and loneliness among divorced adults?

Definitions

Divorced adult: Individual 18 years or older whose marriage is legally dissolved.

Hopelessness: Feeling despair and lack of belief that life can be better than it currently feels (The Jed Foundation, n.d.).

Loneliness: The painful or distressful experience in which one's social relations are perceived as deficient in quality and quantity (Clark et al., 2021; Hutten et al., 2021).

Nervousness: Feeling of timidness or apprehensiveness (Merriam-Webster, n.d.).

Worthlessness: Feeling of hopelessness and uselessness or belief that one has no value (Good Therapy, 2019).

CHAPTER 2

LITERATURE REVIEW

This review examines loneliness in general. Next, demographics such as gender, age, and race and their impact on individuals' level of loneliness are examined. This chapter includes studies on smoking habits and their impact on loneliness. Additionally, studies on access to health care, having a disability, caregiving, and mental health factors and their implications for loneliness are explored.

Loneliness

Loneliness is characterized by feeling alone regardless of who is present, difficulty creating deep connections, and self-doubt (Cigna Healthcare, 2022). Two individuals with the same number of close friends might feel different levels of loneliness due to the difference in their desired relationships. Likewise, two individuals with the same number of close friends might experience different levels of loneliness if they have different perceptions of the quality of those relationships (Barreto et al., 2021). Although loneliness has always greatly affected individuals, the COVID-19 pandemic contributed to the rise in the levels of loneliness (Patulny & Bower, 2022). A cross-sectional study examined the level of loneliness among Germany's residents (Beutel et al., 2017). The study consisted of 15,010 participants aged 35 to 74 years old. The majority (89.5%) of participants reported no loneliness, 4.9% reported slight loneliness, 3.9% reported moderate loneliness, and 1.7% reported severe loneliness (Beutel et al., 2017). In a study of 2,251 adults, emotional loneliness was more prevalent (29.2%) than social loneliness (26.7%). About 13.6% of the sample experienced both types of loneliness (Fierloos et al., 2021).

Demographics and Loneliness

Studies showed that several demographic characteristics are associated with loneliness (Barreto et al., 2021; Choi et al., 2022; Clark et al., 2021; Fierloos et al., 2021; Hutten et al., 2021; Luhmann & Hawkley, 2016; Mullen et al., 2018; Raymo & Wang, 2022; Taylor & Nguyen, 2020). Studies showed various outcomes regarding the relationships between race and loneliness (Choi et al., 2022; Mullen et al., 2018; Raymo & Wang, 2022; Taylor & Nguyen, 2020). A study of 6,469 participants examined the association between depression and loneliness among Black and White individuals (Taylor & Nguyen, 2020). The study sample comprised of 89.08% White respondents and 10.91% Black individuals. Most respondents were not employed (57.7%). The study found that the impact of race on the relationship between loneliness and depression was more significant in older White adults than in older Black adults (Taylor & Nguyen, 2020). Additionally, a study of 310 participants comprised of primarily Caucasian individuals (65.23%) showed that Caucasian participants were 4.7 times more likely to report loneliness than their non-Caucasian counterparts (Choi et al., 2022). In another study that used the UCLA 3-Item Loneliness Scale, Black men had the highest prevalence of loneliness (29%) compared to their White (24%) and Hispanic (22%) male counterparts (Raymo & Wang, 2022). In the same study, Black women also had the highest prevalence of loneliness (33%) compared to their Hispanic (31%) and White (26%) female counterparts (Raymo & Wang, 2022); however, in another study of 1,235 participants that showed divorced respondents are more likely to experience loneliness than married respondents, results showed no significant relationship between race and loneliness (Mullen et al., 2018).

Existing literature revealed inconsistencies in the differences in levels of loneliness across the lifespan (Barreto et al., 2021; Clark et al., 2021; Hutten et al., 2021). Some results showed that loneliness steadily decreases with older age (Barreto et al., 2021). In contrast, other

results showed a U-shaped relationship with loneliness increasing during adolescence,

decreasing in young adulthood, and increasing into middle and older adulthood (Clark et al.,

2021). In a 2021 BBC Loneliness Experiment of 46,054 participants, 19% were divorced and

ranged from 16 to 99 years old, with a mean of 49.7 years old. The study used a quasi-

experimental design and found that younger individuals were more lonely than middle-aged

participants (Barreto et al., 2021). Additionally, middle-aged respondents reported higher rates of

loneliness than older participants. Age had a negative association with loneliness, meaning older

respondents were less lonely than younger individuals (Barreto et al., 2021). Another cross-

sectional study of females (53.0%) revealed that loneliness is prevalent throughout the lifespan

but that there may be different risk factors at different ages. Individuals older than 64 had the

highest prevalence of moderate loneliness, followed by individuals between 30 and 60 years old

(33.2%) and individuals younger than 30 years old (30.7%; Hutten et al., 2021). Findings

suggesting loneliness is more prevalent in older populations may be attributed to the idea that

loneliness is less stigmatized amongst older individuals, making it more likely for them to

accurately report their loneliness (Barreto et al., 2021).

Existing literature also showed mixed results regarding the relationship between gender

and loneliness (Barreto et al., 2021; Clark et al., 2021; Luhmann & Hawkley, 2016). In a study

with respondents from 237 countries, islands, and territories, the sample consisted of 39% males

and included 29.1% single, 31.1% married, and 19% divorced or widowed (Barreto et al., 2021).

Given the large sample size, the study was the first to examine the interplay of age, gender, and

culture with such a diverse sample. This study used a quasi-experimental design and males were

found to have higher rates of loneliness than women ($\beta = -0.08$, $t = -15.73$, $p < .001$; Barreto et al., 2021); however, in another cross-sectional study, men (42%) were less likely to be lonely than women (45%). Regarding marital status and loneliness, those least likely to report loneliness were single (34.4%), followed by married participants (46%), separated or divorced respondents (53.6%), and widowed individuals (79.2%) were the most likely to be lonely (Clark et al., 2021). Additionally, a German study of individuals 17 and older used the UCLA Loneliness Scale to analyze the relationship between gender and loneliness. The study found that females reported higher levels of loneliness ($M = 1.03$, $SD = 0.77$) than males ($M = 0.95$, $SD = 0.71$; Luhmann & Hawkley, 2016). It was also found that the differences in which genders are socialized may influence the differences in their reported loneliness (Barreto et al., 2021). Women are socialized to have more active social lives than men, which may contribute to men's higher rates of loneliness. Studies do not have sufficient data on individuals who do not identify as male or female, and further research is needed to conduct a meaningful analysis of non-binary individuals (Barreto et al., 2021).

Studies showed a negative association between education and loneliness (Clark et al., 2021; Hutten et al., 2021). In a cross-sectional study of 1,009 participants aged 11 and above, results showed that individuals with less education and those who were unemployed had higher rates of loneliness (Clark et al., 2021). In this study, a stratified random sampling process was used. The 11-item De Jong Gierveld Loneliness Scale was used to measure loneliness which yielded a score between 0-11 to indicate loneliness. In this Maltese study, 41.3% of respondents showed moderate levels of loneliness, and 2.1% of individuals reported severe loneliness. Severe levels of loneliness were most prevalent for the age range of 45-54 years, while those aged 20-24 had the lowest rates of severe loneliness (Clark et al., 2021). Another study found that individuals over 60 also showed a negative relationship between education and loneliness.

Individuals with low education were most likely to be lonely (62.2%), followed by middle (20.5%) and high (17.3%; Hutten et al., 2021).

Some additional studies also showed a negative relationship between educational attainment and loneliness (Fierloos et al., 2021; Raymo & Wang, 2022). A study of 2,251 adults showed an association between older age and higher emotional and social loneliness (Fierloos et al., 2021). The mean age of the sample was 79.7 years old, and the sample consisted of 60.4% women. Respondents with tertiary-level education had the lowest prevalence of loneliness among both types of loneliness. Respondents with lower educational levels had higher rates of emotional loneliness. Respondents with primary education or less had the highest prevalence of emotional loneliness (35.1%), followed by secondary education (27.8%) and tertiary education (20.9%); however, the study found that respondents with secondary education had the highest rates of social loneliness (28.8%), followed by primary or less (24.1%) and tertiary (19.9%). Respondents with primary or lower education were 1.82 times more likely to experience emotional loneliness than respondents with tertiary education (Fierloos et al., 2021). Another study showed a negative association between educational level and loneliness. Respondents with less than a high school education had the highest rates of loneliness (34.9%), followed by individuals with a high school education (28.5%) and college education (24.5%; Raymo & Wang, 2022)

Studies found that employment is associated with loneliness (Luhmann & Hawkley, 2016; Mullen et al., 2019). The 2016 German study consisted of primarily unemployed individuals (42.1%), followed by full-time workers (37.2%) and other work statuses (20.6%; Luhmann & Hawkley, 2016). Most of the sample lived with a partner (70.3%), followed by single individuals (21.9%) and respondents not living with their partner (7.8%). Respondents who self-identified as unemployed reported higher levels of loneliness ($M = 1.05$, $SD = 0.81$)

than those who were employed full-time ($M = 0.94$, $SD = 0.68$; Luhmann & Hawkley, 2016).

Additionally, a cross-sectional study consisted of mostly females (63%) and Whites (71%) and

found comparable results (Mullen et al., 2019). The study used the 3-item UCLA Loneliness

Scale ($M = 4.2$, $SD = 1.6\%$), and the majority (45%) of the sample was employed full-time,

followed by part-time (10%) and unemployed (5%). The study found that unemployed

individuals reported significantly higher levels of loneliness (Mullen et al., 2019).

Smoking Habits and Loneliness

The CDC (2021a) reported that disease caused by smoking cigarettes is one of the most

significant public health issues. More than 20 million Americans had died since 1964 when the

first Surgeon General's Report on smoking was released (CDC, 2021a). Roughly 30.8 million

adults smoke in the United States and over 16 million individuals suffer from a smoking-induced

disease (CDC, 2022a). Cigarette smoking is responsible for 1 in 5 deaths in the United States

(CDC, 2022a). The CDC (2021a) found that about 13 out of every 100 adults are current

smokers in the United States. Men (14.1%) are more likely to smoke cigarettes than women

(11%) and the age group most likely to smoke is 45 to 64 years old (14.9%; CDC, 2022a).

Regarding education levels, those with a GED certificate (32%) are most likely to smoke,

followed by those with only some high school (21.5%). Individuals with a graduate degree

(3.5%) were least likely to smoke in the education groups. Those with a disability (19.8%) were

more likely to smoke than those without a disability (11.8%; CDC, 2022a).

Cigarette smoking is prevalent among many vulnerable populations. In a study using the

National Health Interview Survey and the National adult Tobacco (Drope et al., 2018), it was

found that college-educated individuals had the most significant decrease in smoking over the past 50 years. Those with a high school diploma or less (23.1%) are most likely to smoke among the different educational levels. All socioeconomic groups have decreased their smoking habits, but the men from the lowest income group had a 25% decrease, while the highest income men had a 46% decrease. The study found that the American Indian population had the highest smoking prevalence, and the Asian and Latinx populations had the lowest. The disparities may be attributed to the tobacco industry's tactics in advertising and retail locations (Drope et al., 2018).

Due to weak instruments and biased samples, there is limited research on smoking and loneliness (Anjum & Smitha, 2020; Beutel et al., 2017; Wootton et al., 2021). In a study of 15,010 individuals, those who reported current smoking significantly increased with increasing levels of loneliness (Beutel et al., 2017). In this study, only 10.5% of the sample reported feeling lonely, 4.9% of respondents reported slight loneliness, 3.9% scored moderate levels, and 1.7% were severely lonely. Regarding health behavior, the proportion of smokers nearly doubled with increasing levels of loneliness. One fifth (18.5%) of respondents who reported no loneliness were current smokers, while 26.1% of those who reported slight loneliness were current smokers (Beutel et al., 2017). Of those who reported moderate loneliness, 27.4% reported currently smoking, while 31.8% of those with severe loneliness reported smoking. There is over a 13% increase in smokers from those with no loneliness and those with severe loneliness. Strengths of this study include its large sample size and the utilization of standardized self-report instruments. A limitation is that it is a cross-sections study, not permitting causal conclusions (Beutel et al., 2017).

Another study of 511,280 individuals examined the bidirectional causal effect of loneliness, alcohol use, and smoking (Wootton et al., 2021). Observational evidence showed that smoking increases loneliness. The study used Mendelian randomization (MR) to analyze the

causal relationship between loneliness, smoking habits, and alcohol use. The study reviewed

smoking, the number of cigarettes per day, and cessation (Wootton et al., 2021). The results

showed a weak relationship between loneliness causing increased smoking habits. There was

evidence supporting the influence smoking has on increased levels of loneliness. Some

limitations of this study include a weak genetic instrument for loneliness and a possible selection

bias in the sample. The sample was more educated, healthier, and less likely to smoke than the

general population (Wootton et al., 2021).

The findings of one study that used a 1-item measure of loneliness align with overall

research on loneliness, questioning its validity (Beutel et al., 2017); however, further research

should continue to prove its validity by comparing it with alternative loneliness scales.

Additionally, further research should consider the size and quality of social networks among

respondents to accurately assess the effect of social isolation, an essential variable of loneliness

(Beutel et al., 2017). Researchers suggest using stronger genetic instruments in future loneliness

studies. However, since the negative consequences of both smoking and loneliness are well

established in existing literature, researchers recommend addressing the factors simultaneously

with the updated understanding of their interrelatedness (Wootton et al., 2021).

Another study found no significant difference in reported loneliness among smokers and

non-smokers (Anjum & Smitha, 2020). The sample comprised 75 tobacco smokers and 75 non-

smokers. The level of loneliness for smokers ($M = 25.6$) was higher than for non-smokers'

loneliness ($M = 22.36$). However, no significant difference in loneliness between the two groups

was found (Anjum & Smitha, 2020).

Caregiving and Loneliness

Nearly 18 million U.S. individuals were informal caregivers, providing unpaid, in-home assistance for their family or friends in 2015 (Edwards et al., 2020). Caregiving can negatively affect the quality of life for individuals providing care for another person's social or health needs (CDC, 2019). Caregiving can include assisting with everyday responsibilities such as bathing and transportation, managing chronic disease, and providing emotional support. As the recipient's caregiving needs increase, caregivers may experience additional stress. Informal and unpaid caregivers are essential to the long-term care provided in patients' homes. Caregivers' lives can be disrupted in various areas, including the ability to work, social lives, and maintaining physical and mental health (CDC, 2019).

Research reveals that being a caregiver is associated with levels of loneliness (Hutten et al., 2021; Vasileiou et al., 2017). A study on loneliness that categorized the sample into three age groups, under 30, between 30 and 64, and over 64, found a significant, positive correlation between loneliness and caregiving throughout all age groups. Among them, 11.3% of those below 30 years of age reported that their caregiving responsibilities did not burden them compared to 23.5% of those aged between 30 and 64 years. Additionally, 2.6% of the middle age group reported being somewhat burdened by caregiving responsibilities (Hutten et al., 2021).

In another cross-sectional, qualitative study on the loneliness of 16 caregivers, data were analyzed using an inductive thematic analysis to examine the relationship between the role of being a caregiver and the level of loneliness (Vasileiou et al., 2017). Eleven participants were women. The mean age was 63. Eight respondents cared for a spouse, four cared for a parent, three cared for a child, and one cared for a partner. The main themes contributing to the loneliness of these caregivers included shrunken personal space, diminished social interactions, relational deprivations, losses, distancing, powerlessness, and a sense of sole responsibility (Vasileiou et al., 2017). Feelings of loss contributed to their loneliness due to their loved ones experiencing dementia or the loss of freedom to engage in activities and routines that they used to enjoy doing with their loved ones. The sample reported that caregiving roles significantly limited their activities. A limitation is that the study was cross-sectional. Further research should utilize a longitudinal study to examine possible fluctuations in loneliness in different stages of one's caregiving experience, such as entering the role or providing care at the end of life (Vasileiou et al., 2017).

Mental Health and Loneliness

Mental health impacts all ages and affects how individuals think, feel, and behave (CDC, 2021b). Mental health can include emotional, psychological, and social. The CDC (2021b) reports that over half of Americans have a mental illness or disorder in their lifetime. Depression is a common mental illness, and about 80% of those experiencing depression report that their symptoms have caused difficulty with tasks at work, home, or social activities (Brody et al., 2018). Depressive symptoms can include hopelessness and diminished self-worth (Zahn et al., 2015). The U.S. Department of Health and Human Services (2022b) found that about 21 million adults experience at least one depressive episode. Additionally, women (10.5%) were found to have higher rates of depression than men (6.2%). The U.S. Department of Health and Human Services (2022b) also found that those who identify with two or more races and those between the ages of 18 - 25 are most likely to experience depressive episodes.

The CDC (2022b) found that 11.7% of adults experience persistent anxiety symptoms, such as worry and nervousness. Various disorders are associated with anxiety, including panic disorder, phobias, and generalized anxiety disorder (U.S. Department of Health and Human Services, 2022a). The U.S. Department of Health and Human Services reports that anxiety can impair individuals' functioning in employment, education, and socialization. Genetic and environmental factors play a role in anxiety. Some common risk factors include distressing childhood events, living in or experiencing stressful environments, and a family history of mental health disorders. Health issues such as thyroid conditions and substance use can also trigger anxiety (U.S. Department of Health and Human Services, 2022a).

Research reveals a positive relationship between mental health and loneliness (Clark et al., 2021; Hoffmann et al., 2020; Nuyen et al., 2019). A study of 342 participants used the UCLA Loneliness Scale and the Liebowitz Social Anxiety Scale as measures to examine the relationship between anxiety and loneliness amongst individuals in two different age groups: young adults (19-40 years) and older adults (61-89 years; Hoffmann et al., 2020). The study analyzed how age moderates the relationship between characteristics of social anxiety, such as fear of social interactions, and characteristics of loneliness, such as minimal intimate relationships. The study did not find any differences in personal loneliness among the two different age groups but did find age-group differences among non-intimate loneliness levels such as "social others" and "affiliative environment" (Hoffmann et al., 2020). Social others refer to the loneliness that stems from having fewer people to turn to than desire. Affiliative environment refers to the loneliness that stems from lacking a feeling of belonging. Intimate loneliness refers to a feeling deprived of the quantity or quality of close friends. The older adults were found to have higher non-intimate loneliness than the younger participants (Hoffmann et al., 2020). The study also found that older adults had less social anxiety than younger participants. The relationship between social anxiety and loneliness was more remarkable for older adults than younger ones. A limitation of this study is that it is cross-sectional, limiting the ability to suggest a causal relationship (Hoffmann et al., 2020).

Additionally, the results may not represent older adults in institutionalized settings such as nursing homes (Hoffmann et al., 2020). Including more vulnerable participants, such as those recently widowed or those unable to leave their residence, may also increase the sample's representativeness. Regarding the strengths of this study, it was the first to contribute to research on older adults that included both social anxiety and intimate loneliness (Hoffmann et al., 2020).

One nationally representative Dutch study of individuals ($N = 4{,}007$) aged 18 to 64 used stratified random sampling to examine the bidirectional relationship between common mental disorders (CMDs) and loneliness (Nuyen et al., 2019). The study did a follow-up interview 3 years after the initial baseline interview. Of the individuals who did not report loneliness during the first interview, nearly 8% had a moderate CMD, and over 3% had a severe CMD. At the 3-year follow-up, almost 10% of this subgroup reported loneliness. Of the respondents who reported loneliness at baseline, more participants (15.3%) reported a severe CMD than those who reported a moderate CMD (12.1). The study found that severe CMD during initial interviews increased the likelihood of loneliness, but moderate CMD did not (Nuyen et al., 2019). Additionally, the study found that severe CMD in those who initially reported loneliness increased the likelihood of persistent loneliness during the 3-year follow-up. The differences in loneliness due to the severity of CMD may be attributed to biological, psychological, or social factors. These factors can include coping skills, self-esteem, or health choices. The large sample size and use of standardized instruments were strengths of this study. However, the study may only represent the Dutch population (Nuyen et al., 2019).

Another study that addresses the relationship between not feeling optimistic about their lives has higher rates of loneliness than those who feel confident about their lives (Clark et al., 2021). Most (74.2%) of those who do not feel optimistic about life reported loneliness, while only 39.8% of those with a positive mindset felt lonely. Additionally, of those who reported having "terrible" coping abilities, 79.4% reported feeling lonely, while only 30.8% of those who have "very good" coping abilities experienced loneliness. The lack of considering cultural impacts on individuals was noted as a limitation in this study (Clark et al., 2021).

Several studies found that additional longitudinal research, rather than cross-sectional, can better understand the causal relationship between mental health and loneliness (Clark et al., 2021; Hoffmann et al., 2020; Nuyen et al., 2019). Even the research conducted over 3 years may be limited due to not accurately accounting for an individual's history of mental health before the interviews (Nuyen et al., 2019). The representativeness of research regarding mental health and loneliness might have affected the findings (Clark et al., 2021; Hoffmann et al., 2020). Further research on mental health and loneliness is warranted (Clark et al., 2021; Hoffmann et al., 2020; Nuyen et al., 2019).

Disabilities and Loneliness

Sixty-one million adults in the United States have a disability, and 1 in 3 has an unmet healthcare need due to the cost (CDC, 2020a). For those 65 years and above, 2 out of 5 individuals have a disability. One in every 4 women has a disability, and 2 out of every 5 American Indians have a disability. About 33% of adults aged 18- 44 do not have a usual healthcare provider, 13.7% of those with a disability have difficulty with mobility, 10.8% have a cognitive disability, 5.6% of individuals with a disability are deaf, and 4.6% have severe difficulty with vision (CDC, 2020a).

Research showed that having a disability is associated with higher rates of loneliness (Burholt et al., 2017; Clark et al., 2021; Hutten et al., 2021; Kasikci & Dayapoglu, 2020). A study of 3,314 participants analyzed the relationship between disabilities and loneliness (Burholt et al., 2017). The sample was 54% female, the average age was 74.6, and 61.7% of participants were married. The study used the six-item De Jong Gierveld Scale to measure the participants' loneliness level and the Mini-Mental State Examination (MMSE) to measure the participants' cognitive functioning (Burholt et al., 2017). The Modified Townsend Disability Scale was used to measure the severity of participants' disabilities. One fourth (25.3%) of the sample scored between 2 and 6 on the loneliness scale, indicating that about one quarter were lonely. The study found that disability was associated with poor life outcomes. Additionally, the study found a significant total effect of disability on loneliness and a weaker, but still significant, direct effect (Burholt et al., 2017).

In a cross-sectional study on loneliness, stratified random sampling was used, and there was a final sample of 1,009. The study used the 11-item De Jong Gierveld Loneliness Scale to measure the participants' loneliness, 41.3% of the sample reported moderate loneliness, and 2.1% reported severe loneliness ($M = 2.65$; Clark et al., 2021). Participants with a disability were more likely to report loneliness (57.3%) than those without a disability (42.3%). Another cross-sectional study used data from 52,341 participants from a survey conducted by the regional public health services in the province of Limburg. Three different age groups were examined: younger than 30 years, between 30 and 64 years, and older than 64 years (Hutten et al., 2021). It looked at seven risk factors of loneliness, including demographics, socioeconomic status, physical disability, mental health, societal participation, frequency of social contact, and network type. Several risk factors of loneliness include disability, inadequate financial resources, and lower educational attainment. More specifically, the study found that disability was a risk factor during early and late adulthood but less in middle adulthood (Hutten et al., 2021). Another study conducted Chi-square tests and found that having a disability was associated with loneliness (Clark et al., 2021).

A descriptive study of 92 participants diagnosed with multiple sclerosis aimed to examine the levels of disability and loneliness. The sample consisted of individuals from a Turkish hospital's neurology polyclinic (Kasikci & Dayapoglu, 2020). Disability levels were measured using the Brief Disability Questionnaire, the Self Care Ability Scale to measure self-care engagement, and the UCLA Loneliness Scale to assess loneliness levels. The patients' age range was 18 to 60 years old, and the sample consisted of about 71% females and about 66% married individuals. Regarding disability levels, 32.6% reported none, 22.8% reported minimal levels, 26.1% reported moderate, and 18.5% reported severe levels ($M = 50.14 \pm 13.37$). There was a statistically significant moderate, positive correlation, $r = 0.408$ ($p < .001$), between disability levels and loneliness. The study found a negative, strong correlation between self-care and loneliness $r = -0.662$ ($p < 0.001$). A limitation of this study is that the findings may only be generalized to the population at the Turkish hospital (Kasikci & Dayapoglu, 2020).

Diabetes and Loneliness

The CDC (2020b) estimated that over 34 million Americans had diabetes in 2018. Diabetes was found to be prevalent among more men than women. Additionally, individuals with less than a high school education (13.3%) had higher rates of diabetes than those with a high school (9.7%) or college education (7.5%; CDC. 2020b). Research shows that individuals diagnosed with diabetes are at an increased risk for loneliness (Corno & Burns, 2022; Dziedzic et al., 2021). A longitudinal study utilized data from the Health and Retirement Study to study diabetes, functional limitations, and loneliness among middle aged and older adults (Corno &

Burns, 2022). Individuals with diabetes often have functional limitations such as difficulties

completing daily tasks. The sample was mostly White (74.98%), and the average amount of time

participants had diabetes was 10.4 years. The study found that loneliness and functional

limitations had bidirectional associations (Corno & Burns, 2022). A cross-sectional Polish study

on loneliness had a sample of 248 diabetic participants. The sample had a mean age of 57.9

(Dziedzic et al., 2021). The sample mostly report low levels of loneliness (47%), followed by

moderate (36%), high (13%) and (3%). The single, diabetic respondents ($M = 41.05$, $SD = 13.5$)

were more lonely than their counterparts in a relationship ($M = 37.08$, $SD = 10.68$; Dziedzic et

al., 2021).

Conclusion

In conclusion, loneliness can vary based on factors such as the perceived quality of

relationships versus the desired quality of relationships (Barreto et al., 2021). There are also

distinct types of loneliness including social loneliness and emotional loneliness (Fierloos et al.,

2021). Research showed that a wide variety of attributes could impact levels of loneliness.

Regarding race, some research indicates that White individuals are more likely to report

loneliness (Choi et al., 2022; Taylor & Nguyen, 2020), while other studies found that Black

individuals were more likely to report loneliness (Raymo & Wang, 2022). Research also showed

some variation in the relationships between age and loneliness (Barreto et al., 2021; Clark et al.,

2021; Hutten et al., 2021). Ultimately, while loneliness can vary throughout the lifespan, it is

present at all ages. Those unemployed and individuals with low education achievement also

showed high levels of loneliness (Clark et al., 2021; Fierloos et al., 2021; Hutten et al., 2021;

Raymo & Wang, 2022).

Research on cigarette smoking and loneliness varies, and a causal relationship has not been established clearly (Anjum & Smitha, 2020; Beutel et al., 2017; Wootton et al., 2021). Being an informal caregiver is also a risk factor for increased levels of loneliness (Hutten et al., 2021; Vasileiou et al., 2017), and individuals with disabilities are at risk for high rates of loneliness (Clark et al., 2021; Hutten et al., 2021; Kasikci & Dayapoglu, 2020). Additionally, feelings of depression and mental health factors are associated with loneliness (Clark et al., 2021; Hoffmann et al., 2020; Nuyen et al., 2019). Diabetes was also found to be associated with higher rates of loneliness (Corno & Burns, 2022; Kobos et al., 2021). Research lacks extensive data on loneliness among divorced adults, so continued research is necessary.

CHAPTER 3

METHODOLOGY

Design

This research uses secondary data with a descriptive, quantitative methodology to examine factors contributing to loneliness among divorced adults. The factors included demographics, smoking habits, healthcare hardship, and mental health. The secondary data was acquired from the California Health Interview Survey (CHIS; 2020). The survey was administered by collaborating agencies including the UCLA Center for Health Policy Research, the California Department of Health Care Services, and the California Department of Public Health. The CHIS survey was administered via telephone and web (CHIS, 2020).

Sampling

The CHIS interviewed California residents on various health and demographic topics. The sample is selected using an address-based sampling (ABS) frame to ensure that the model is representative of the population (CHIS, 2020). The ABS is chosen from the United State Postal Services' Computerized Delivery Sequence file because it has thorough coverage of the household population. Individuals are invited to complete the survey through mail invitations, which include a call-in number. Households with a listed phone number are also asked to complete the survey (CHIS, 2020). To address commonly unrepresented demographic groups, the CHIS targeted homes of Korean, Vietnamese, Latino, and Spanish-speaking individuals, those without citizenship, and those with low educational attainment. The CHIS is administered to several age groups, with some questions tailored to the specific age group. The age groups include 0-11 years old (children), 12-17 years old (adolescents), and 18 years and older (adults;

CHIS, 2020). This study used a nonprobability, purposive sampling procedure to create a sample of adults who self-identify as divorced.

Data Analysis

The Statistical Package for Social Science (SPSS) 28.0 was used to analyze the secondary data from the CHIS. Univariate, descriptive statistics for variables are used to explore respondents' demographic characteristics. One-way ANOVA and independent group t-tests are used to test the research questions.

Social Work Ethics

Improving the overall well-being of individuals is part of the primary mission of the social work profession (National Association of Social Workers [NASW], 2022). This study aligns with the task by contributing to research that can provide insight into how to improve the lives of divorced individuals. According to the NASW (2022), the profession emphasizes sensitivity to diversity in culture and ethnicity. This research uses data from CHIS, which intentionally attempts to include households of Korean, Vietnamese, Latino, and Spanish-speaking individuals and those without citizenship or with low educational attainment.

Additionally, participants in the California Health Interview Survey provided informed consent after being introduced to the interviewer, UCLA, and survey sponsors, the survey's purpose, and an understanding of the personal and voluntary aspects of the study (CHIS, 2020). Following these explanations, the interviewee answered if they would like to participate in the survey and implied consent if they continued with the survey. The participants were allowed to skip questions or terminate the interview at any time. Due to the sensitive nature of some questions, any variables that could be considered sensitive or identifiable are not included in the Public Use Files to protect the participants' anonymity and privacy (CHIS, 2020).

Social Work Relevance to Integrated Health

Smoking habits, healthcare hardships, and mental health are all present in the integrated healthcare setting. All three factors contribute to loneliness among divorced adults. Continuing research on these factors can aid in improving individuals' well-being in integrated healthcare settings (Clark et al., 2021; Hutten et al., 2021; Wootton et al., 2021). From a macro perspective, social workers must continue researching the divorced population to understand better the unique negative consequences of smoking, health care hardships, and mental health of this population to best advocate for their needs and improve overall health outcomes. With a better understanding of these factors, social workers can use a more informed approach while assisting their clients in navigating adversity in the integrated healthcare setting.

CHAPTER 4

RESULTS

Univariate Results

Personal Characteristics

Table 1 displays the personal characteristics of the adults who identified themselves as divorced. The study sample mainly consisted of Whites (70.9%), followed by Native /Indigenous/other races (9.3%), Asians (7.5%), Latinos (7%), and African Americans (5.3%). The sample's age ranges included 18- to 54-year-olds (19.1%), 55- to 64-year-olds (20.8%), 65- to 74-year-olds (30.8%), and 75+-year-olds (29.3%). The study sample comprised 3,443 females (70.4%) and 1,449 males (29.6) who identified themselves as divorcees. Less than half of the sample were employed (41.4%), and the rest were unemployed/retired/not looking for work (58.6%). Additionally, the educational levels of the sample consisted of less than high school (4.1%), high school (14.6%), some college (34.5%), and a bachelor's or higher degree (46.8%).

Smoking Characteristics

Table 2 shows the cigarette smoking habits of the sample. Most of the sample never smoked regularly (57.2), followed by those who quit smoking (35.2%) and those who currently smoke (7.6%). Regarding frequency by day, most participants did not smoke at all (92.4%), followed by those who smoked every day (5.3%) and those who smoked some days (2.3%).

TABLE 1. Personal Characteristics, *N* = 4,892

Category	*f*	%
Race/Ethnicity		
Latino	343	7
Asian	369	7.5
African American	260	5.3
White	347	70.9
Native/Indigenous/Two or More Races	453	9.3
Age		
18-54 yrs	933	19.1
55-64 yrs	1018	20.8
65-74 yrs	1506	30.8
75+ yrs	1435	29.3
Gender		
Male	1449	29.6
Female	3443	70.4
Work Status		
Employed	2026	41.4
Unemployed/Retired/Not Looking for Work	2866	58.6
Education Level		
Less Than High School	202	4.1
High School	715	14.6
Some College	1687	34.5
College Degree or More	2288	46.8

TABLE 2. Smoking Habits, *N* = 4,892

Category	*f*	%
Current Smoking Habit		
Currently Smokes	372	7.6
Quit Smoking	1724	35.2
Never Smoked Regularly	2796	57.2
Smoking Frequency		
Every day	259	5.3
Some Days	113	2.3
Not At All	4520	92.4

Caregiving Characteristics

Table 3 shows the caregiving characteristics of divorced adults. Within the past year,

most of the sample did not provide caregiving services to family or friends (74.8%), followed by those who did provide caregiving services to family or friends within the past year (25.2%).

The divorced adults experienced various levels of financial stress due to caregiving

responsibilities, including not at all stressful (14.3%), a little stressful (6.2%), somewhat

stressful (3.3%), and highly stressful (1.4%). The study sample consisted of 1,027 divorced

adults (21%) who did not suffer from physical or mental health problems related to their

caregiver responsibilities, and 205 divorced adults (4.2%) did suffer physically or mentally due

to their caregiver responsibilities. Regarding the divorced adults' relationships to the care

recipients, 8.6% provided care to a friend or other relative, followed by a parent (8.4%), a

spouse or partner (3%), a child (2.7%), a sibling (2.2%), and a grandparent (0.3%). The sample

consisted of 7.5% of divorced adults who lived with their care recipient within the past 12

months, and 17.7% of divorced adults did not live with their care recipient. Additionally, 5.4%

of divorced adults provided care for recipients who have Alzheimer's or dementia, while 19.8%

of divorced did not provide care for those specific illnesses.

TABLE 3. Caregiver Characteristics, $N = 4,892$

Category	f	%
Provide Care to Family or Friend Within the Past Year		
Yes		
No	1232	25.2
	3660	74.8

Mental Health Characteristics

Table 4 shows the mental health characteristics of the sample. Most divorced adults

reported feeling not at all hopeless in the past 30 days (69.8%), followed by those who felt

hopeless a little of the time (17.9%), some of the time (9.5%), most of the time (2.1%) and all of

the time (.07%). Regarding feeling nervous in the past 30 days, 38.1% of the divorced adults

reported feeling not at all nervous, followed by those who reported feeling nervous a little of the time (35.1%), some of the time (20.7%), most of the time (4.8%), and all of the time (1.2%). Most of the divorced adults reported feeling not at all restless (44.3%) or feeling restless a little of the time (31.7%), followed by some of the time (18.4%), most of the time (4.3%), and all of the time (1.3%). Most of the divorced adults reported feeling not at all depressed (76.5%), followed by feeling depressed a little of the time (13.7%), some of the time (7.4%), most of the time (1.8%), and all of the time (0.6%). Additionally, most of the participants reported feeling not at all worthless (81.3%), followed by all of the time (10.9%), most of the time (5.1%), some of the time (1.7%), and a little of the time (1.0%).

Disabilities and Diabetes

Table 5 shows the disability and diabetic characteristics. One tenth (10.7%) of the divorced adults reported being blind or deaf, and 14.7% of the sample was diagnosed with diabetes.

Loneliness by Personal Characteristics

Table 6 shows the relationships between demographic characteristics and loneliness among divorced adults. A one-way ANOVA showed a statistically significant association between divorced adults' race and loneliness ($F = 53.742$, $df = 4$, $p < .001$). Among the divorced adults, Whites ($M = 2.9888$, $SD = 2.49226$) had the highest level of loneliness, followed by African Americans ($M = 2.2846$, $SD = 2.34227$), Asians ($M = 2.0488$, $SD = 2.34702$), Native and Indigenous adults ($M = 2.0044$, $SD = 2.43135$), and Latinos ($M = 1.3994$, $SD = 2.17527$). An independent samples t-test showed a statistically significant relationship between education and loneliness ($t = 4.746$, $df = 3$, $p = 0.003$). Divorced adults with less than a high school diploma had the highest level of loneliness ($M = 2.9307$, $SD = 2.53437$), followed by those who were with a high school education ($M = 2.9245$, $SD = 2.33891$), some college ($M = 2.7018$, $SD =$

2.52356), and college degree or more ($M = 2.5608$, $SD = 2.52071$). An independent samples t-test showed a significant association between employment status and loneliness ($t = -39.421$, $df = 4890$, $p < 0.001$). Divorced adults who were employed ($M = 1.2182$, $SD = 2.11445$) had lower levels of loneliness than those who were unemployed, retired, or not looking for work ($M = 3.70$, $SD = 2.22$). An independent samples t-test showed that the relationship between gender and loneliness only approached significance ($t = 1.413$, $df = 4,890$, $p = 0.079$). A strong, positive correlation was found between age and loneliness ($r = .698$, $p < .001$).

Loneliness by Smoking Habits

Table 7 shows the relationship between cigarette smoking and loneliness. A one-way ANOVA showed a statistically significant association between current smoking habits and loneliness ($F = 67.864$, $df = 2$, $p < .001$). Divorced adults who quit smoking had the highest level of loneliness ($M = 3.2268$, $SD = 2.4238$), followed by those who never smoked regularly ($M = 2.4102$, $SD = 2.47712$) and those who currently smoke ($M = 2.1452$, $SD = 2.57301$).

Loneliness by Caregiving Characteristics

Table 8 shows the relationship between caregiving and loneliness. An independent samples t-test indicated a statistically significant relationship between providing caregiving services and loneliness ($t = -6.78$, $df = 4,890$, $p < 0.001$). Divorced adults who were caregivers had lower levels of loneliness ($M = 2.2622$, $SD = 2.5633$) than those who were not caregivers ($M = 2.8178$, $SD = 2.46215$).

Loneliness by Mental Health

Table 9 shows the correlation results between mental health and loneliness. Table 9 also shows the correlation results between age and loneliness. The correlation between hopelessness and loneliness was not significant ($r = .004$, $p = .794$). There was a statistically significant weak, negative correlation between nervousness and loneliness ($r = -.058$, $p < .001$). There was also a

statistically significant weak, negative correlation between restlessness and loneliness ($r = -.082$,

$p < .001$). The correlation between depression and loneliness was not statistically significant ($r =$

$-.015$, $p=.297$). Additionally, the correlation between worthlessness and loneliness was not

statistically significant ($r = .007$, $p = .640$).

TABLE 4. Mental Health Characteristics, $N = 4,892$

Category	f	%
Felt Hopeless For The Past 30 Days		
All The Time	35	0.7
Most Of The Time	105	2.1
Some Of The Time	463	9.5
A Little Of The Time	876	17.9
Not At All	3413	69.8
Felt Nervous For The Past 30 Days		
All The Time	60	1.2
Most Of The Time	237	4.8
Some Of The Time	1011	20.7
A Little Of The Time	1719	35.1
Not At All	1865	38.1
Felt Restless For The Past 30 Days		
All The Time	64	1.3
Most Of The Time	211	4.3
Some Of The Time	899	18.4
A Little Of The Time	1549	31.7
Not At All	2169	44.3
Felt Depressed For The Past 30 Days		
All The Time	29	0.6
Most Of The Time	88	1.8
Some Of The Time	362	7.4
A Little Of The Time	672	13.7
Not At All	3741	76.5
Felt Worthlessness In The Past 30 Days		
All The Time	534	10.9
Most Of The Time	251	5.1
Some Of The Time	83	1.7
A Little Of The Time	47	1.0
Not At All	3977	81.3

TABLE 5. Disability and Diabetes Characteristics, *N* = 4,892

Category	*f*	%
Blind/Deaf or Has Severe Vision/Hearing Loss		
Yes	522	10.7
No	4370	89.3
Diagnosed with Diabetes		
Yes	721	14.7
No	4171	85.3

TABLE 6. Loneliness by Personal Characteristics, *N* = 4,892

Category	*N*	*M*	*SD*	*t/F*	*df*	*p*
Ethnicity						
Latino	343	1.399	2.175	53.742	4	<.001
Asian	369	2.048	2.347			
African American	260	2.284	2.342			
White	3467	2.988	2.492			
Native American/Indigenous/Two or More	453	2.004	2.431			
Education Level						
< High School	202	2.930	2.534	4.746	3	0.003
High School	715	2.924	2.338			
Some College	1687	2.701	2.523			
College Degree or More	2288	2.560	2.520			
Gender						
Male	1449	2.755	2.572	1.413	4890	0.079
Female	3443	2.645	2.467			
Work Status						
Employed	2026	1.218	2.114	-39.421	4890	<0.001
Unemployed/Retired/Not Looking for Employment	2866	3.709				

TABLE 7. Loneliness by Smoking Habits, _N_ = 4,892

Category	N	M	SD	t/F^{df}	p
Current Smoking Habit		2.14		67.86	<.00
Currently Smokes	372	5	2.573	4 2	1
Quit Smoking	172 4	3.22 6	2.423		
Never Smoked	279 6	2.41 0	2.4771 2		

TABLE 8. Loneliness by Caregiving Characteristics, _N_ = 4,892

Category	N	M	SD	t/F
Provided Caregiving in the Last 12 Months				
Yes	1232	2.262	2.563	-6.78
No	147	5.33	4.317	

TABLE 9. Correlation Matrix Loneliness & Mental Health, _N_ = 4,892

	1	2	3	4	5	6	7
Felt Hopeless (1)	1						
Felt Nervous (2)	.515**	1					
Felt Restless (3)	.468**	.597**	1				
Felt Depressed (4)	.666**	.443**	.450**	1			
Felt Worthless (5)	.647**	.403**	.405**	.644**	1		
Age (6)	-.193**	-.227**	-.250**	--.167**	-.152**	1	
Loneliness (7)	-.004	-.058**	-.082**	-.015	.007	.698**	1

**. Correlation is significant at the 0.01 level (2-tailed)

Loneliness by Disabilities and Diabetes

Table 10 shows the relationship between disabilities and loneliness. An independent samples _t_-test indicated a statistically significant relationship between being blind or deaf and loneliness (_t_ = 12.092, _df_ = 4890, _p_ < 0.001). Blind or deaf divorced adults had higher levels of loneliness (_M_ = 3.91, _SD_ = 2.36122) than participants who did not have those disabilities (_M_ = 2.5307, _SD_ = 2.47298). An independent samples _t_-test showed a statistically significant relationship between diabetes and loneliness (_t_ = 9.382, _df_ = 4,890, _p_ < 0.001). Diabetic participants had higher levels of loneliness ($M = 3.4771$, $SD = 2.51326$) than those who did not

have diabetes ($M = 2.5397$, $SD = 2.47123$).

TABLE 10. Loneliness by Disability and Diabetes, $N = 4,892$

Category	N	M	SD	t/F	df	p
Blind or Deaf						
Yes	522	3.91	2.361	12.092	4890	<.001
No	4370	2.530	2.474			
Diagnosed with Diabetes						
Yes	721	3.477	2.513	9.382	4890	<.001
No	4171	2.539	2.471			

CHAPTER 5

DISCUSSION

Summary of Findings

This study examined how demographic characteristics, smoking habits, caregiving factors, mental health factors, and disabilities are associated with loneliness among 4,892 divorced adults sampled from the CHIS (2020) survey. The study found that White divorced adults were more lonely than non-White divorced participants. The research also found that divorced participants with a college degree were less lonely than divorced participants with less education. The study found that loneliness increased with older age. Additionally, divorced participants who were unemployed and those who self-identified as female had higher rates of loneliness than their employed or male counterparts.

The study found that divorced adults who quit smoking cigarettes were lonelier than those who never smoked and those who currently smoke. The study also found that divorced adults who provided caregiving services were less lonely than those who did not provide caregiving services. Divorced adults who reported nervousness were less lonely than those who were not. Additionally, divorced adults who reported restlessness were less lonely than those who were not restless. The research also found that divorced adults were lonelier if they were blind or deaf. Divorced adults were also more likely to be lonely if they had diabetes.

Comparison of Study Findings with Prior Research

Previous studies found conflicting results regarding the relationship between race and loneliness (Choi et al., 2022; Mullen et al., 2018; Raymo & Wang, 2022; Taylor & Nguyen, 2020). Some researchers showed that White individuals are lonelier than their non-White counterparts (Choi et al., 2022; Taylor & Nguyen, 2020). Another research showed that Black individuals are more likely to report loneliness than White or Hispanic individuals (Raymo &

34

Wang, 2022). Additionally, one study showed no significant relationship between race and loneliness (Mullen et al., 2018). The current study found that White divorced adults were lonelier than non-White divorced participants.

Prior research found mixed results regarding the relationship between age and loneliness (Barreto et al., 2021; Clark et al., 2021; Hutten et al., 2021). Some studies showed that loneliness increased with age (Barreto et al., 2021; Clark et al., 2021). Another researcher showed that middle-aged individuals are lonelier than older individuals (Hutten et al., 2021). The current study found that older divorced adults were lonelier than younger ones.

Previous literature showed mixed results regarding the relationship between gender and loneliness (Barreto et al., 2021; Clark et al., 2021; Luhmann & Hawkley, 2016). One study found that males were lonelier than females (Barreto et al., 2021); however, other studies found that women were lonelier than males (Clark et al., 2021; Luhmann & Hawkley, 2016). The current study found that divorced men were lonelier than divorced women.

Previous studies showed a negative association between education and loneliness, indicating that individuals with less education had higher rates of loneliness (Clark et al., 2021; Fierloos et al., 2021; Hutten et al., 2021; Raymo & Wang, 2022). The current study found results that support previous research. The participants with less than a high school education were lonelier than those with a high school diploma, some college education, and a college degree.

Consistent with previous research that showed employment is negatively associated with loneliness (Luhmann & Hawkley, 2016; Mullen et al., 2019), this study found that divorced individuals who were unemployed, retired, or not looking for employment were lonelier than employed respondents.

Existing research revealed varying results regarding the relationship between smoking (Anjum & Smitha, 2020; Beutel et al., 2017; Wootton et al., 2021). Some studies showed a positive relationship between smoking and loneliness (Beutel et al., 2017; Wootton et al., 2021). However, another study found no significant difference in the level of loneliness between smokers and non-smokers (Anjum & Smitha, 2020). The current study found that the divorced adults who quit smoking scored highest on loneliness, followed by divorced adults who never smoked and those who currently smoke.

Previous studies found caregivers were lonelier than non-caregivers, but the level of loneliness varied based on reasons for loneliness and age (Hutten et al., 2021; Vasileiou et al., 2017). However, this study found that divorced caregivers were less lonely than non-caregivers.

Existing literature showed a positive relationship between mental health factors and loneliness, suggesting that individuals with mental health disorders or symptoms are more likely to experience loneliness than those who do not have a disorder (Clark et al., 2021; Hoffmann et al., 2020; Nuyen et al., 2019). The current study found no statistically significant correlation between hopelessness, worthlessness, depression, and loneliness. The present study did not align with previous research and found a weak, negative correlation between nervousness and loneliness and restlessness and loneliness.

Previous research showed that having a disability is associated with higher rates of loneliness (Burholt et al., 2017; Clark et al., 2021; Hutten et al., 2021; Kasikci & Dayapoglu, 2020). The current study was consistent with previous research and found that divorced respondents with disabilities such as blindness, deafness, and diabetes are lonelier than their able-bodied counterparts.

Existing literature found a positive relationship between mental diabetes and loneliness (Corno & Burns, 2022; Kobos et al., 2021). The current study also found that divorced participants who were diabetic were lonelier than their nondiabetic counterparts.

Implications for Social Work Practice

The divorced population requires continued attention from social workers because of the immense adverse effects of divorce, including issues in financial affairs, parenting, and emotions (Sbarra et al., 2015). The primary mission of social workers is to improve the overall well-being and assist vulnerable, oppressed, and impoverished communities in getting their needs met (NASW, 2022). The core values that social workers use as a guide while serving individuals, families, and communities include service, social justice, dignity and worth of the person, importance of human relationships, integrity, and competence. Regarding service, social workers must prioritize applying their professional skills to help those in need and are encouraged to engage in some pro-Bono services (NASW, 2022). To meet the core value of service when serving divorced adults, social workers can facilitate accessible, community-based support groups for divorced adults and their families. One effective modality that social workers can use while promoting group therapy for divorced adults is the Post-Divorce Psychological Support Program, which has been shown to effectively improve divorced adults' adjustment levels (Karadeniz Özbek & Demir, 2022).

To adhere to the core value of social justice, which includes increasing access to information and resources, social workers can collaborate with community-based attorney services to increase the population's knowledge of the legal process of divorce (NASW, 2022). By doing so, social workers can facilitate more informed decision-making for individuals who are getting divorced. A study on a support group for divorced men showed that legal education could foster individuals' interactions in formal legal institutions throughout the divorce process (McMorrow, 2016). By forming this collaboration, social workers can also provide early interventions by connecting individuals with emotional support services while they navigate the divorce process. The study on divorced men also showed that skills needed throughout the legal education process include developing personal insight and relationships (McMorrow, 2016). However, there is a lack of resources addressing divorce's harmful financial effects on women. Divorce may reinforce the social issues of economic inequality between men and women (Raley & Sweeney, 2020). The growing disparity calls for more attention to the financial well-being of divorced women.

To honor the dignity and worth of the person, social workers must provide respectful services that are mindful of cultural differences to empower individuals in addressing their own needs (NASW, 2022). Considering critical race theory (CRT), social workers need to reflect on the intersectionality, or the intersection of the many identities held by clients, to genuinely honor the dignity and worth of individuals (Capper, 2015). While serving divorced adults, social workers can honor their dignity and worth in a culturally appropriate manner by allowing the client to share their personal experience within their culture and aid in processing the feelings or possible stigma associated with divorce in the client's culture while helping clients to build their own set of coping skills and supports. This process also aligns with the counter-story telling component of CRT and will allow divorced adults to share unique experiences (Capper, 2015). Regarding the importance of human relationships, social workers are expected to understand the vitality of relationships in change and maintaining well-being (NASW, 2022). While serving divorced adults, social workers can engage as a partner and use the self to aid the strengthening of divorced adults' relationships. To honor the social work value of integrity, social workers must maintain the knowledge of social work ethics and act following them. Social workers must also serve clients only within their areas of competence (NASW, 2022). To adhere to integrity and competence, social workers must enhance their knowledge of divorced adults, their outcomes, and risk factors or refer clients to appropriate services.

Implications for Future Research

Due to the inconsistent findings between the demographics of divorced adults and loneliness, future research is warranted to understand better the demographic risk factors that impact divorced adults' loneliness. Further understanding of these risk factors can help social workers identify protective factors regarding loneliness among divorced adults. Additionally, further research can continue to explore the relationships between caregiving and loneliness among divorced adults and the relationship between mental health factors and loneliness among divorced adults to clarify the conflicting results found between this current study and previous research. Further analysis can better explore the differences in risk factors among divorced adults versus married or single adults to understand the risk factors unique to divorced adults. Lastly, future research can aim to better represent the level of loneliness among divorced adults by creating a more extensive, inclusive, and culturally appropriate loneliness scale and by including members of the LGBTQ+ community.

Limitations of the Study

The use of non-probability purposive sampling may have caused results that do not accurately represent the overall population, which may result in poor external validity regarding the study's findings. One major limitation of the data used in this study is that only California residents with a residential address were used, which leaves out all individuals in institutionalized or group residences and those unhoused. This limitation is harmful as it may cause the data not to represent those living in poverty and those unable to live outside the institutional setting. Additionally, since the CHIS collected the data in 2020, the COVID pandemic may have impacted the respondents' reported level of loneliness (CHIS, 2020). Alternative purposes for collecting this data, which did not aim to explore the loneliness of divorced adults, may have influenced this study's findings.

Conclusion

Understanding the loneliness among divorced adults is vital in aiding their improved well-being and perceived quality of life. This quantitative study analyzed the various risk factors of loneliness for divorced adults, including demographics, smoking habits, caregiving, mental health factors, and disabilities. Further research can continue to explore the factors contributing to loneliness among divorced adults, which may allow for more appropriate interventions and to examine protective factors. The current study indicates that divorced adults are a unique population that is not equally affected by risk factors for loneliness to the factors found in general people. Consequently, social workers should continue to explore the risk factors specific to this population to better aid them in reducing their loneliness.

APPENDIX

DATA RETRIVAL FORM

California Health Interview Survey 2019-2020

Adult Questionnaire

Version 1.18

August 24, 2021

Personal Characteristics

1. 'QA20_A4' [AA2A] - Are you between 18 and 29, between 30 and 39, between 40 and 44, between 45 and 49, between 50 and 64, or 65 or older?

   A. Between 18 and 29

   B. Between 30 and 39

   C. Between 40 and 44

   D. Between 45 and 49

   E. Between 50 and 64

   F. 65 or older

2. 'QA20_A6' [AD66B] - Do you currently describe yourself as male, female, or transgender?

   A. Male

   B. Female

3. 'QA20_A18' [AA5F] - Which do you most identify with?

A. Latino

B. American Indian or Alaskan Native

C. Asian

D. Black or African American

E White

F. Both/All/Multiracial

4. The next questions are about your employment. How many hours per week do you usually work at all jobs or businesses? If you do not work, enter 0 (zero) _____ Hours [HR: 0-95]

5. 'QA20_A21' [AH43] - Are you now married, living with a partner in a marriage-like relationship, widowed, divorced, separated, or never married?

A. Married

B. Living with partner

C. Widowed

D. Divorced

E. Separated

F. Never married

6. 'QA20_G19' [AH47] - What is the highest grade of education you have completed and received credit for?

A. No Formal Education

B. Grade School

C. High School Or Equivalent

D. 4-Year College Or University

E. Graduate Or Professional School

F. 2-Year Junior Or Community College

G. Vocational, Business, Or Trade School

7. QA20_G27' [AG10] - Do you usually work?

01 Yes

02 No

03 Looking for work

Smoking Habits

8. 'QA20_C6' [AE15A] - Do you now smoke cigarettes every day, some days, or not at all?

A. Every day

B. Some day

C. Not at all

Caregiving Characteristics

9. 'QA20_J58' [AJ87] – Now we'd like to ask about care giving. Some people provide short-term or longterm help to a family member or friend who has a serious or chronic illness or disability. This may include help with things they cannot do for themselves. During the past 12 months, did you provide any such help to a family member or friend? This may include help with baths, medicines, household chores, paying bills, driving to doctor's visits or the grocery store, arranging for medical and support services, or just checking in to see how they are doing

A. Yes

B. No

Mental Health Characteristics

10. 'QA20_E2' [AJ29] About how often during the past 30 days did you feel ....nervous?

A. All of the time

B. Most of the time

C. Some of the time

D. A little of the time

E. None of the time

11. 'QA20_E3' [AJ30] - ... hopeless?

A. All of the time

B. Most of the time

C. Some of the time

D. A little of the time

E. None of the time

12. 'QA20_E7' [AJ34] - ... worthless?

A. All of the time

B. Most of the time

C. Some of the time

D. A little of the time

E. None of the time

Loneliness Scale Questions

13. 'QA20_F26' [AF107B] - The next questions are about how you feel about different

aspects of your life. For each one, please tell me how often you feel that way. First, how

often do you feel that you lack companionship?

Is it...

A. Hardly ever

B. Some of the time

C. Often

14. 'QA20_F27' [AF108B] - How often do you feel left out? Is it...

A. Hardly ever

B. Some of the time

C. Often

15. 'QA20_F28' [AF109B] - How often do you feel isolated from others? Is it...

A. Hardly ever

B. Some of the time

C. Often

Disabilities and Diabetes

16. QA20_D4' [AD50] - Are you blind or deaf, or do you have a severe vision or hearing

problem?

A. Yes

B. No

17. 'QA20_B8' [AB22] - {Other than during pregnancy, has/Has} a doctor ever told you that

you have diabetes or sugar diabetes?

A. Yes

B. No